Guided reading notes
by Kate Ruttle (series editor)

Trackers level 5: Tiger tracks

Numbers Count

Genre: non-fiction **Text type:** magazine **Author:** Sarah Fleming	

Numbers are all around you, but do you ever stop to think what they mean? Find out different ways in which numbers count.

High frequency words	Useful long vowel phonemes	Content words and Tricky words
called, come, does, four, keep, last, light, more, new, only, page, same, square, thing, think, today, used, way, world, would, write	'ai' in *always, away, based, dates, equator, games, grain, greatest, label, names, page, place, play, player, same, say, take, today, trade* 'ie' in *by, cried, divide, find, hide, infinite, light, nine, try, why* 'or' in *Augustus, also, before, corner, for, fort, four, important, more, war, water, York, your*	*ancient, Augustus, calculator, decimal, dividing, Egyptian, emergency, equator, mathematical, multiply, reference, questionnaire*

Guided reading

The aim of this series is to encourage children to read for meaning. This booklet provides page-by-page notes suggesting a variety of ways to do this.

Guided reading could be covered in three stages:

1 Introduce the book
2 Read the book
3 Revisit the book

For guidance on how to go through these stages, see the back cover.

Main text is in white panels. This is the text that the children should try to read independently. It contains a high proportion of high frequency and phonically regular words.

Other texts present a higher level of challenge, but most children should be able to read it with some support.

Independent reading

This book can be used for independent reading. To help children read for meaning, use some of the ideas from the 'Read the book' notes on the back cover.

Asking questions

Encourage the children to ask questions of you and of each other as both asking and answering questions develops comprehension. Throughout their reading, use the italicised questions in this booklet to make children think about the meaning of both individual words and bigger text.

Phonics and high frequency words

In the 'Follow on' boxes there is information about phonically regular words on the pages. If children get stuck on these words, they can be encouraged to 'sound them out'. The high frequency words listed are all from the *Trackers* Tiger Tracks high frequency word list (see Teacher's Guide) and are words that children need to learn to recognise.

For notes on phonics and high frequency words plus general information on how to teach these, see *Trackers* Teacher's Guide for levels 5 and 6.

How to use this booklet

This booklet is intended to support children in guided reading sessions. On each page in this booklet there is a page map, a diagram of the pupils' page which represents a double-page spread (two pages) in the pupil's book. However, on page 3 of this booklet there might be information about pages 1–3 of the pupil's book. Page 14 includes information about pupil book pages 22–24. On the page map, the page numbers (folios) refer to pages in the pupil's book.

The page map is annotated with these boxes:

Heading

Each new topic is introduced by a heading. New themes in the topic are introduced by subheadings.

Main text boxes

Any potentially challenging words will be identified in the initial 'vocabulary check'. Strategies for reading these words are suggested in the follow on section. These include questions and ideas you can use to monitor children's understanding. Use these as a menu of suggestions rather than as a set list of questions.

Questions you could ask the children are written in italics.

Secondary text

All other text on the pages is secondary text. In general, notes are not included about these boxes, because the expectation is that children will be supported as they read them. These contain supplementary information or questions.

Illustrations

The illustrations are often not referred to in the notes, but children should be encouraged to spend time considering them.

Developing comprehension skills

On page 15 there are some comprehension questions which will require the children to think beyond the scope of a double-page spread. These are consistent with the assessment focuses in SATs papers and include:

★ retrieval of detail (SATs assessment focus 2);
★ inference and interpretation (SATs assessment focus 3);
★ structure and organisation of text (SATs assessment focus 4);
★ writer's uses of language (SATs assessment focus 5);
★ writer's purpose and viewpoint and the overall effect of the text (SATs assessment focus 6).

SATs assessment focus 1 refers to the decoding strategies children use. Opportunities for assessing these are given in the Follow on section on every double page.

Developing speaking and listening

Use the making meaning suggestions on each double page spread to develop speaking and listening skills. These questions, and others in the 'Main text boxes', are often open-ended and support children as they develop their ideas and understanding through talk and discussion.

The main features of the text

Use the information on this page of the booklet to draw children's attention to the specific features of the text type used in the book. As their reading skills develop, it is important that children understand how different text types are structured as this will help them read more effectively and also to understand how texts work when they are writing.

Numbers Count is a magazine text which contains different kinds of texts including:
★ *non-chronological report*
★ *dialogue*
★ *narrative*
★ *instructions.*

Help the children to identify each of the text types considering for each one:
★ *Text purpose:* what is the function of each short text?
★ *Text structure:* how is the text structured? Is the order in which the text is written important to its meaning?
★ *Sentence and word level features:* consider tense, formality of language, use of jargon etc.

Pages 2 and 3

1 Main text – on the contents page
★ Ask the children to consider the question. The numbers may or may not mean anything to them.
★ Read the numbers aloud yourself, using vocabulary like *Double '0' 7*; *Nineteen thirty nine to nineteen forty five*. Do the numbers mean more to the children now?

2 Heading
★ vocabulary check: *meaningful*
★ Discuss what a *meaningful* number is. *Are all numbers meaningful to someone?*

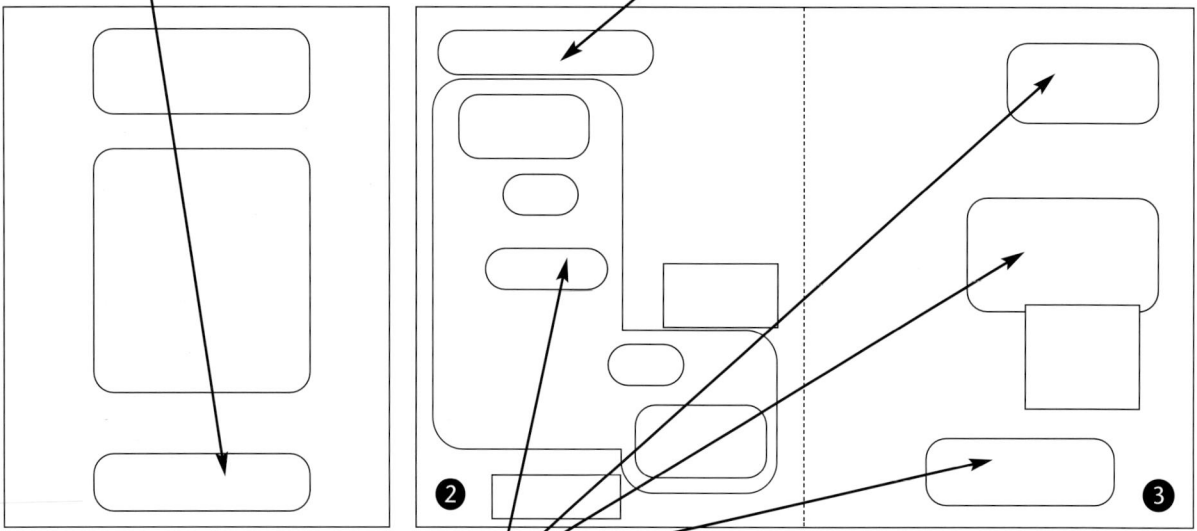

3 Main texts and pictures
★ vocabulary check: *emergency, terrorist, special*
★ Read all the numbers and the meanings given to them in the book. *Are these the same meanings that you thought of?*

Follow on

Tricky words
★ *emergency* (Ask the children to split the word into syllables: *e-mer-gen-cy.*)
★ *terrorist* (Teach base word *and* forming suffix *–ist*: *terror + ist.*)
★ *special* (The tricky bit is the pronunciation of *cial* as 'shul'. Split into syllables: *spe-cial.*)

Words and sentences
★ *What is the text type here and what are its main features?* (answer: report text – present tense, non-chronological, impersonal)

Making meaning
★ *Which numbers are special in your life?* (e.g. birthday, house number, phone number, lucky number)

Pages 4 and 5

4 Heading
★ Ask the children to predict what this page is likely to contain, based on the heading. What usually follows *'think of a number'* or *'pick a card'* etc.?

6 Main texts
★ This page explains the trick by explaining how a simplified version would work.
★ *Who is the child talking to here?*

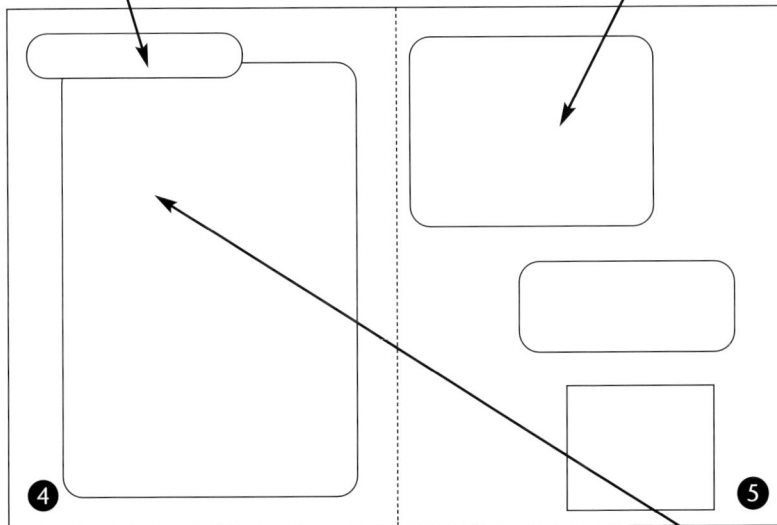

5 Main text
★ **vocabulary check:** *multiply, divide*
★ Make sure that the children know the convention for reading a comic strip like this. They need to recognise the difference between speech and thought bubbles.

❹ ❺

Follow on

Tricky words
★ *multiply, divide* (Ask the children to split the words into syllables: *mul-ti-ply, div-ide.*)

Words and sentences
★ Look at the use of the contracted forms *here's* and *it's*. Can the children tell you the full form each time? Discuss the tone of a text that includes contracted forms, is it more formal or informal?

Making meaning
★ *Why does the child on page 5 give a simplified trick, rather than explaining the original trick more fully?*

Pages 6 and 7

7 Heading
★ vocabulary check: *brief*
★ *What does a 'brief history' mean?*

9 Star fact
★ Read this secondary text with the children. Can they suggest answers to the question?

8 Main text
★ vocabulary check: *Ancient, Egyptians, symbols*
★ Help the children to read the secondary text at the bottom of page 6. It's important that they understand that the numbers are written right to left.
★ *Can you explain how to work out which Ancient Egyptian numbers you are looking at?*

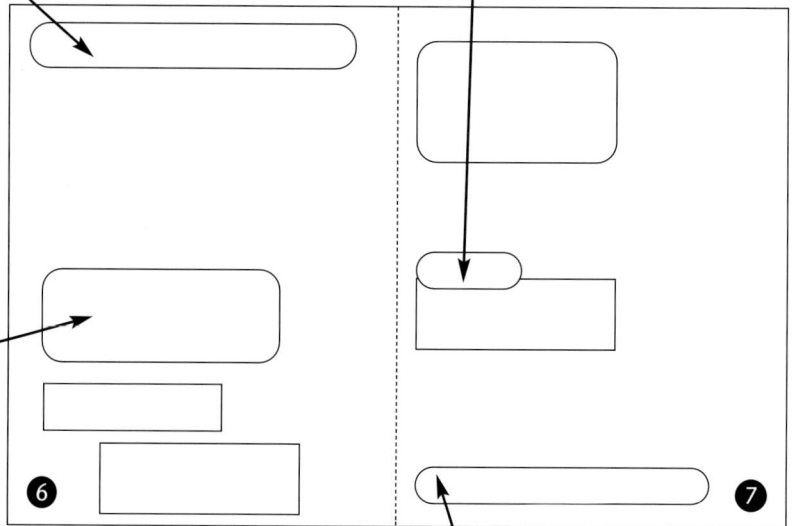

8A Answer box
★ Introduce the convention that in answer boxes, the solution to a puzzle may be written upside down.

Follow on

Tricky words
★ *ancient* (The tricky bit is the pronunciation of *cient* as 'shunt'. Split into syllables: *an-cient*.)
★ *Egyptians* (Teach base word *and* adjective forming suffix *ian* and plural *s*: *Egypt + ian + s*.)
★ *symbols* (Ask the children to split the word into syllables: *sym-bols*.)

Making meaning
★ *Do you think the Ancient Egyptian way of writing numbers is clearer or more difficult than ours?*

Pages 8 and 9

10 Main texts

★ *Why isn't there a heading on this page?* (answer: it's a continuation of the topic from the previous page)
★ *Is the Roman way of writing numbers more familiar than the Ancient Egyptian? Which do you think is easier?*

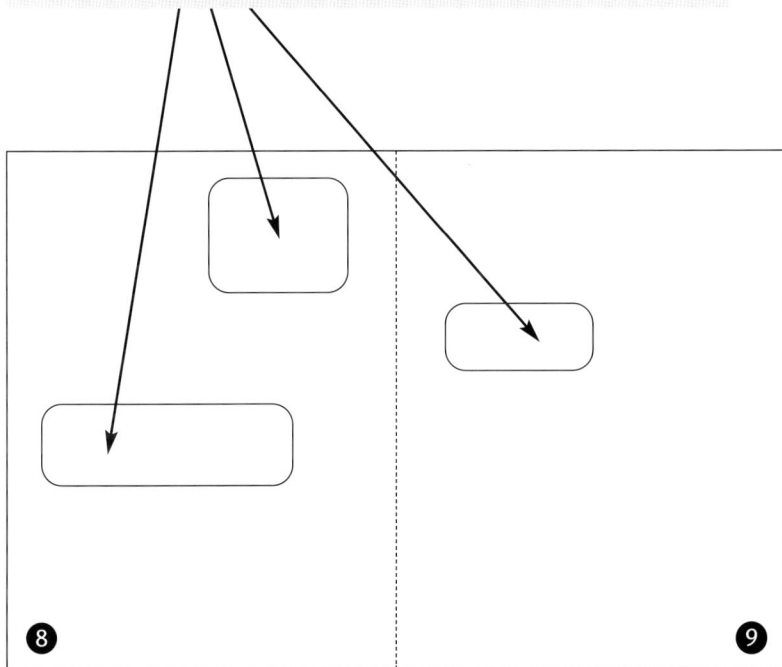

❽ ❾

Follow on

Words and sentences

★ *Which words on the page introduce questions?* Discuss different kinds of questions: questions which require information as part of the answer, and questions to which the answer is *yes* or *no. How does the first word in a question tell you what is expected as an answer?*

Making meaning

★ *How many ways can you think of in which Roman numbers are different from Ancient Egyptian numbers?*

Pages 10 and 11

12 Main text

★ *Which of the other number systems is the Chinese number system most like?*
★ *Why do you think the symbols for number one are so similar?*

11 Main text

★ **vocabulary check:**
thousand
★ *Why is there no heading again?*
★ *Is the Indian system older or more recent than the Roman or the Ancient Greek?* (answer: more recent than the Greek; about the same age as the Roman)

❿ ⓫

Tricky word

★ *thousand* (Ask the children to split the word into syllables: *thou-sand*.)

Words and sentences

★ *Find all the words on the page containing the letter c. How many different ways is it pronounced?* (answer: 'k' in *coin, come* and *Arabic*; 'ch' in *Chinese*; 'sh' in *special*)

Making meaning

★ Discuss why it is called a *system* of numbers. *What is a system?* ('a set of things that work together; an organised way of doing something' a definition from the *Oxford Primary Dictionary*)

Pages 12 and 13

14 Main texts
★ *Have you ever used tally marks? When?*

13 Heading
★ *What do you think this page will be about?*

16 Heading
★ **vocabulary check:** *electronic*
★ *What is an electronic number?* (answer: a number made on an electronic device like a calculator, alarm clock or timer)

17 Main text
★ **vocabulary check:** *calculator*
★ *Why do you think calculator numbers are made using light bars?*

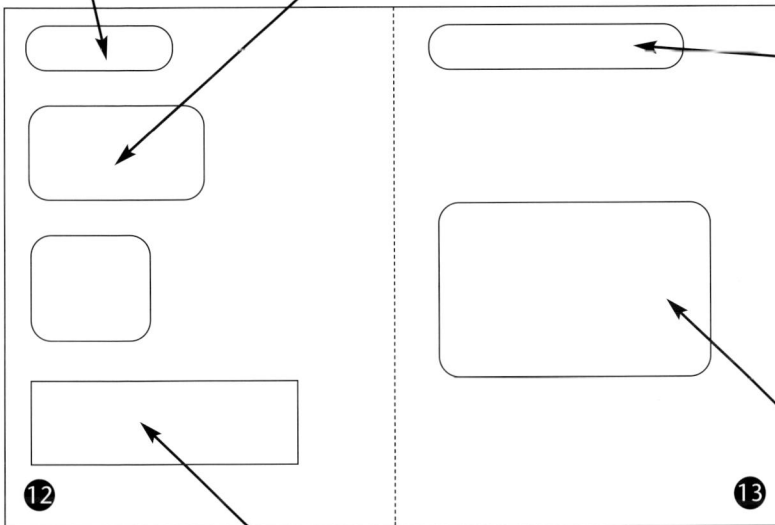

15 Table
★ *Why are tally marks used here? Why might it be easier to use tally marks rather than numbers if you are trying to keep count of something?*

Follow on

Tricky word
★ *electronic* (Ask the children to split the word into syllables: *el-ec-tro-nic*.)

Words and sentences
★ *Why do you think light bars are called light bars?*

Making meaning
★ *Could you write the whole alphabet on the same seven light bars? Which letters would be tricky?*

Pages 14 and 15

18 Heading

★ vocabulary check: *battleships*
★ *What is this page going to be about?*
★ If there is time, let the children play the game. By letting them play, the instructions will make more sense and you can find out if there are any missing instructions that you and the children need to add (see related PCM in Teacher's Guide 3).

21 Main text

★ vocabulary check: *reference, swapping*
★ The children will need to know that when giving grid references the horizontal reference is given before the vertical one.
★ In their pairs, let Player A and Player B each read the lines that refer to them and check that the game is making sense.

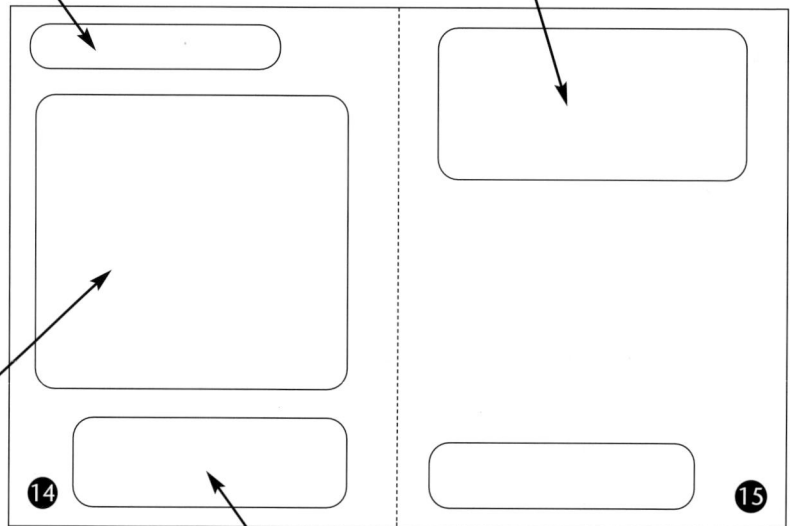

19 Main text and picture

★ vocabulary check: *axis*
★ *What kind of text type is this? How do you know?*

20 Main text

★ In their pairs, the children will need to decide who is player A and who is player B.

Follow on

Tricky words

★ *reference* (The tricky bit is the usually silent syllable *e*: ref-(e)-rence.)
★ *swapping* (The tricky bit is the pronunciation of *wa* as 'wo'. Treat as base word *swap + ing.*)

★ *battleships* (Ask the children to separate the compound word into its components: *battle + ship.*)

Making meaning

★ Ask the children what they think the aim of this game is.

Pages 16 and 17

22 Heading
★ vocabulary check: *mighty*
★ *What is a mighty big number?*

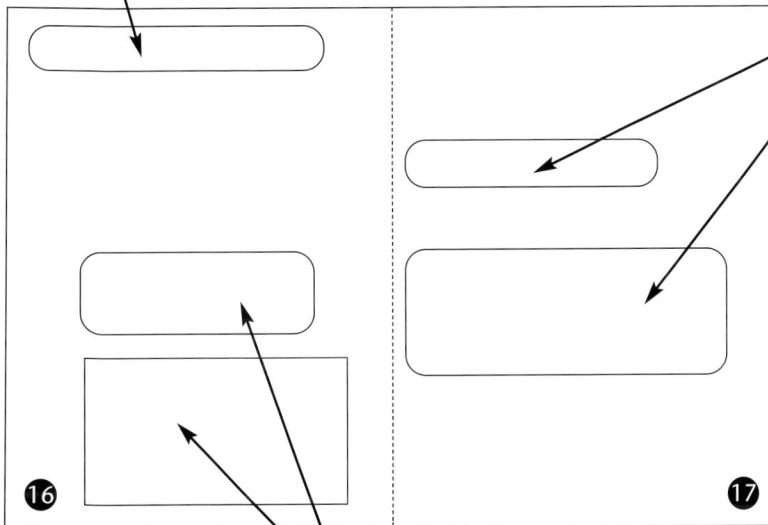

24 Main texts
★ This text explains the reason that the ruler couldn't fulfil the mathematician's wishes.
★ Help the children to pronounce the big numbers. If a trillion is a million times a million then it would look like 1,000,000,000,000. So the number of grains on the last square would be over 9 million trillion. That's a lot of rice!

23 Main text
★ vocabulary check: *mathematician, chessboard, double*
★ *How many squares are there on a chessboard?* (64)
★ *Does this seem like a reasonable request to you?*

Follow on

Tricky words
★ *mighty* (Teach base word and adjective forming suffix *y*: *might + y*.)
★ *mathematician* (The tricky bit is pronouncing *c + ian* as 'shon'. Split into syllables: *math-e-mat-i-cian*.)

★ *chessboard* (Ask the children to separate the compound word into its components: *chess + board*.)
★ *double* (The tricky bit is pronouncing *ou* as 'u': split into syllables: *dou + ble*.)

Making meaning
★ *Do you think that the mathematician was trying to trick the ruler, or do you think he was surprised to realise what he had done?*

Pages 18 and 19

25 Heading

★ **vocabulary check:** *infinity*
★ *Can you really go beyond infinity?* No! Explain to the children that 'infinity' means going on forever without ever stopping, so it's not possible to go beyond it. (The quotation is a popular one from the Disney film *'Toy Story'*.)

26 Main texts

★ Ask the children to read the number aloud. How do they know when to say 'thousand' and when to say 'point'?

27 Main text

★ Make sure that the children understand the link between the pictures all showing one third, and the calculation one divided by three = one shared into three equal parts = one third. This infinite number is the only way you can show a fraction on a calculator. Do the children know that it's called a decimal fraction?

18

19

> **Follow on**

Tricky word

★ *infinity* (Ask the children to split the word into syllables: *in-fin-i-ty*.)

Words and sentences

★ Explore the words *infinite and infinity*. Look inside the words for the word 'finite' which means 'with an end'. The prefix *in* means 'not'. Can the children tell you what the suffix *y* does here?

Making meaning

★ *Why do you think we usually write numbers with as few zeros as is necessary?*

Pages 20 and 21

30 Subheading
★ Why is this a subheading, not a new heading?

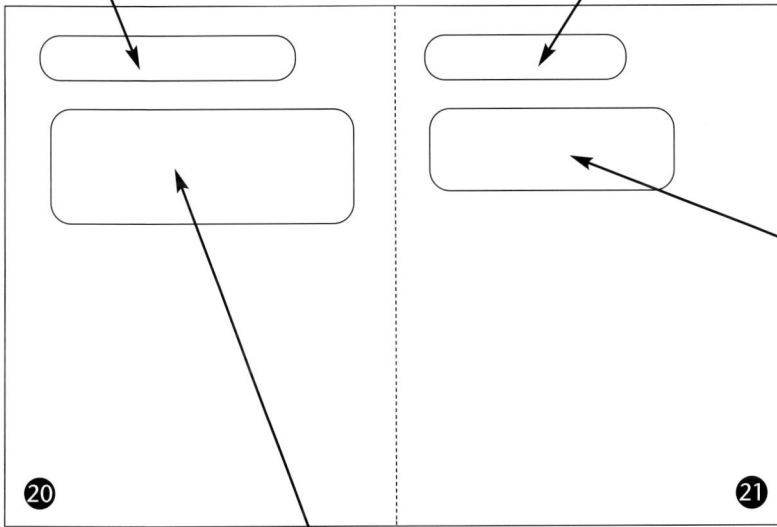

28 Heading
★ Which text type should we be able to predict from a heading like this?

31 Main text
★ What information does this text give you?

29 Main text
★ Which text type is this?
★ What is the aim of the text?

Follow on

Words and sentences
★ Look at the use of singular and plural forms of the words *number* and *grid*. Point out that it is crucial in this text that no mistakes are made with singular and plural forms or the meaning would be confused.

Making meaning
★ Which features of an instructional text can the children identify?

Pages 22, 23 and 24

34 Main texts
* ★ **vocabulary check:** *Kenya, Eastings, Northings, equator*
* ★ Help the children to recognise that using Eastings and Northings is much the same as using ordinary co-ordinates, like the ones they used for battleships. You give a two-digit horizontal number first, then a two-digit vertical number.

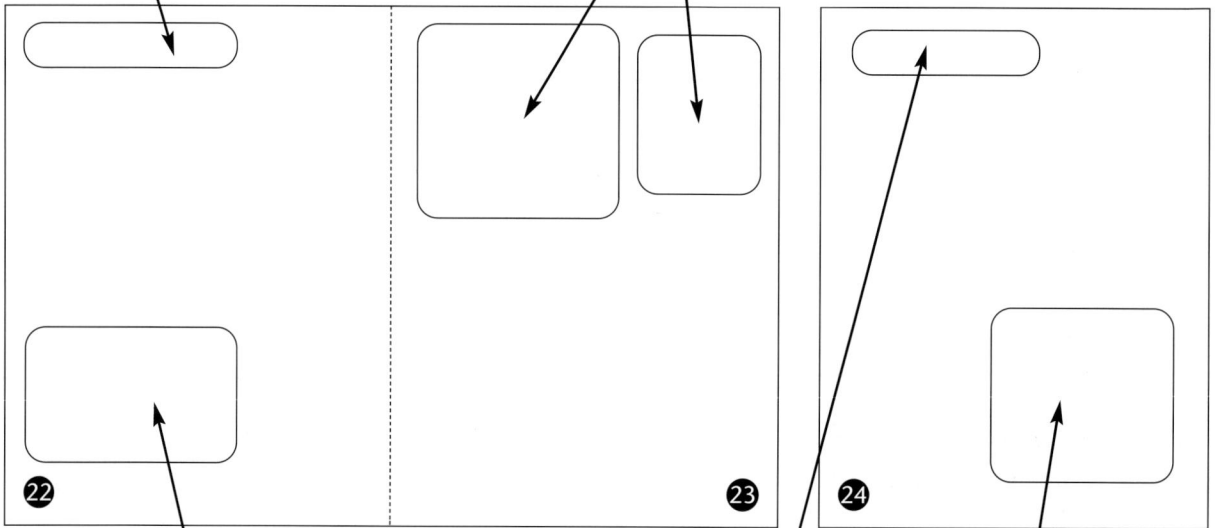

32 Heading
* ★ *What have numbers got to do with maps?*

33 Main text
* ★ *How do you think numbers give you all this information?*

35 Heading
* ★ *Do you know what 'Bonnie' means?* (answer: It is a word used mainly by people who are Scottish and means beautiful.)

36 Main text
* ★ The children will need to use the information they learned on the previous page to provide the grid references.

Revisit the book

★ These questions are intended to make the children think about what they have understood from reading the book.

★ They are not intended to be used as a 'test', nor is it anticipated that children should answer all the questions.

★ First, ask the children to think back and try to answer the questions from memory. Then ask them to find the evidence in the text by finding words or pictures to support their answers.

Retrieval of detail

★ *What can the number 999 mean?* (page 2)

★ *How many symbols did the Ancient Egyptians have to make all the numbers to 999?* (page 6)

★ *How many light bars are needed for each electronic number?* (page 13)

★ *When you give a grid reference, do you give the horizontal or the vertical number first?* (page 15)

★ *In the number 4,321 what is the value of 3?* (page 18)

★ *What kind of information can numbers give you on maps?* (page 22)

Inference and interpretation

★ *Why does the title Think of a Number immediately let you know that a trick is about to be performed?*

★ *Which number system is our number system most like?*

★ *Why are tally marks useful?*

★ *About how many times can you double the number one before you reach a thousand?*

★ *How do you know the value of a digit?*

Structure and organisation of text

★ *How many different kinds of text type did you find in the book?*

★ *Was it tricky reading a mixture of text types?*

Author's uses of language

★ *Is the language in this book formal or chatty and informal? Why?*

Author's purpose and viewpoint and the overall effect of the text

★ *What is this book about? What is the author trying to make the reader do or think?*

1 Introduce the book

★ *What do you think this book is going to be about?* Discuss title, blurb and cover images.

★ *What do you already know about numbers? Jot down what you know and any questions you have.*

★ *How does this book work?* Talk about the overall 'shape' of the book. Use the contents page and point out the book is a mixture of information, games, tricks and stories.

★ *Look at the way each page is set out.* Point out:
  – Headings
  – Main text
  – Secondary text
  – Definition boxes
  – Illustrations.

2 Read the book

★ As the children read, use questions and guidance on the spread-by-spread notes in this booklet, pages 4–14, and the questions children asked in the introductory session. Children can read either just main text, or they can attempt some of the more challenging secondary text.

★ Encourage the children to spend time considering the pictures – they can learn a lot from 'reading the pictures'.

★ At the end of the session, talk about what the children have found in response to the questions you asked.

3 Revisit the book

★ *Have your questions been answered?* Remind children of the questions they asked in the first session. Discuss which have been answered and ask the children why they think some of the questions may not have been answered.

★ *If another group were to read this book, which questions should they be asked to think about?* Encourage the children to re-read parts of the book independently to think about appropriate questions.

★ *How did you read the 'tricky words'?* Focus on tricky words and discuss children's strategies for decoding them.

Follow on

Use these for '5 minute' session beginnings or endings, or to focus children's attention on word, sentence or text-level issues.

★ **'Tricky words'** suggests strategies for decoding words identified in the main text as being potentially challenging.

★ **'Words and sentences'** focuses on issues to do with vocabulary choice, punctuation, grammar and text layout.

★ **'Making meaning'** draws attention to bigger questions that arise from the text or pictures and help to develop comprehension.

OXFORD
UNIVERSITY PRESS

© Oxford University Press
First published 2004

www.OxfordPrimary.com

Numbers Count!

Contents

Sarah Fleming

007, 999, 1939–1945, 9/11

What do these number mean to you?

OXFORD

UNIVERSITY PRESS

Special numbers

The special numbers on the contents page could mean …

007
James Bond

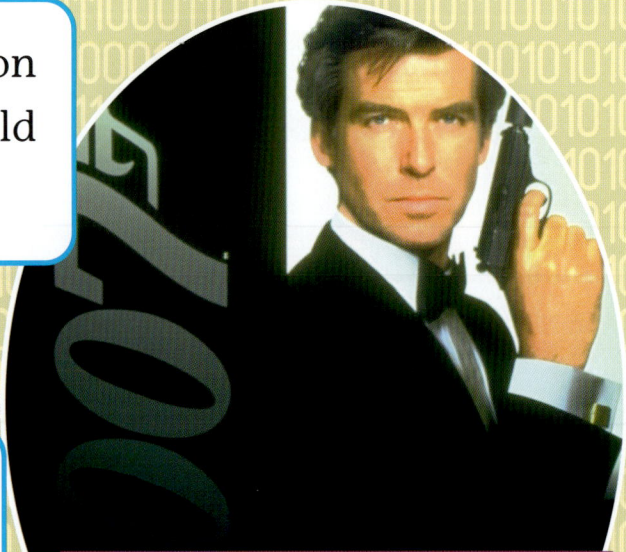

Ian Fleming wrote a series of books about a British spy, James Bond. Bond's secret spy number was 007.

999
The number to dial in an emergency.

On mobile phones you can also dial 112 in an emergency.

1939–1945

The dates of the Second World War.

9/11

The Twin Towers of the World Trade Centre in New York, USA, fell down after a terrorist attack on the 11th of September, 2001.

This day is called "9/11" because in the USA the month (9) is written before the day (11).

911 is also the number of the American emergency services.

Some numbers mean special things just to you.

Think of a number

Think of a number between 1 and 9.

I'll choose 6.

B Multiply it by 4.

6 x 4 = 24

C Then divide by 2.

24 ÷ 2 = 12

D Next add 9.

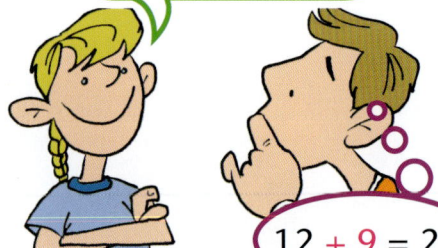

12 + 9 = 21

E Take away your first number. What have you got?

21 − 6 = 15

F 15!

Now, I take away 9. Your first number was 6.

How does this trick work?
Well, here's a simple trick that works the same way.

- Think of a number between one and ten.
- Add four.
- What number have you got?

To find the answer all I do is take away four from the number you gave me.

The trick on page 4 works the same way, only it has more steps and so it's harder. Try it on a friend.

Try this one on a friend:

- Think of a number between one and ten.
- Multiply by six.
- Divide by three.
- Add seven.
- Take away your first number and what have you got?

To work out what your friends first number was take away seven from the number they tell you.

A brief history of numbers

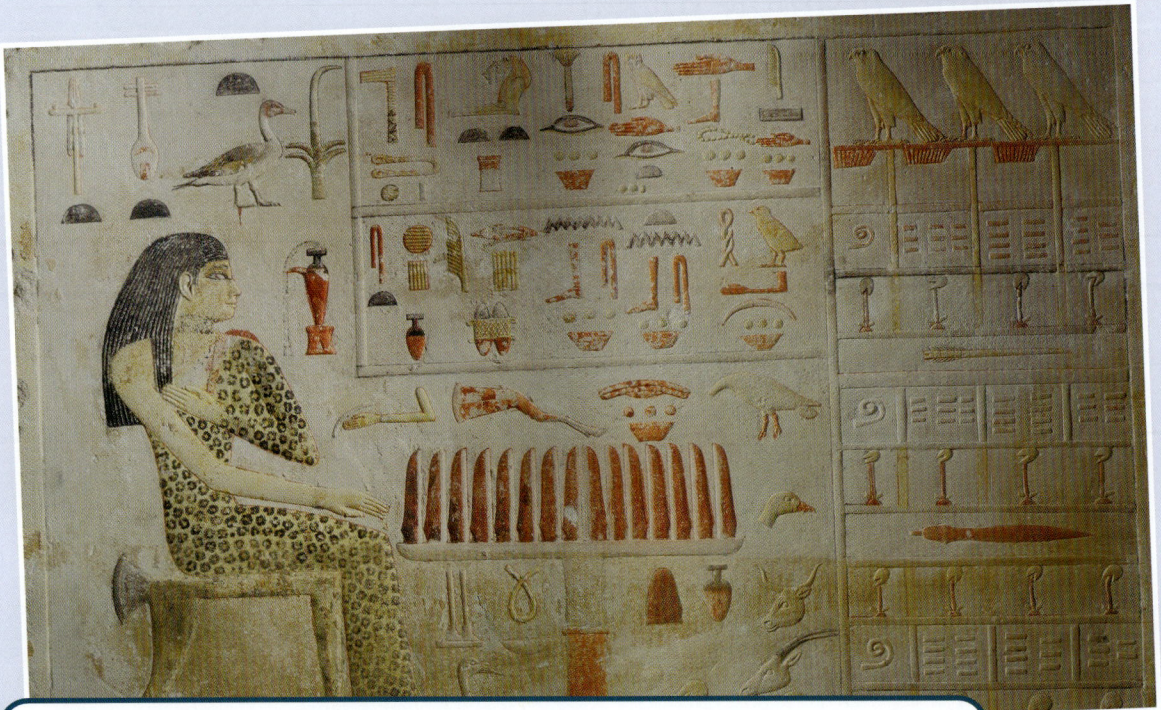

The Ancient Egyptians only had three symbols to make all the numbers up to 999.

| for one (1)

∧ for ten (10)

⑨ for one hundred (100)

So to make 11 you would write |∧

The Egyptians wrote from right to left, and they wrote their numbers that way too. Can you see that the 'ten' symbol to the right of the 'one' symbol?

What numbers are these ?

a |||∧

b ||∧∧𝓈

What are these numbers in Ancient Egyptian numbers ?

c 76

d 203

Answers below

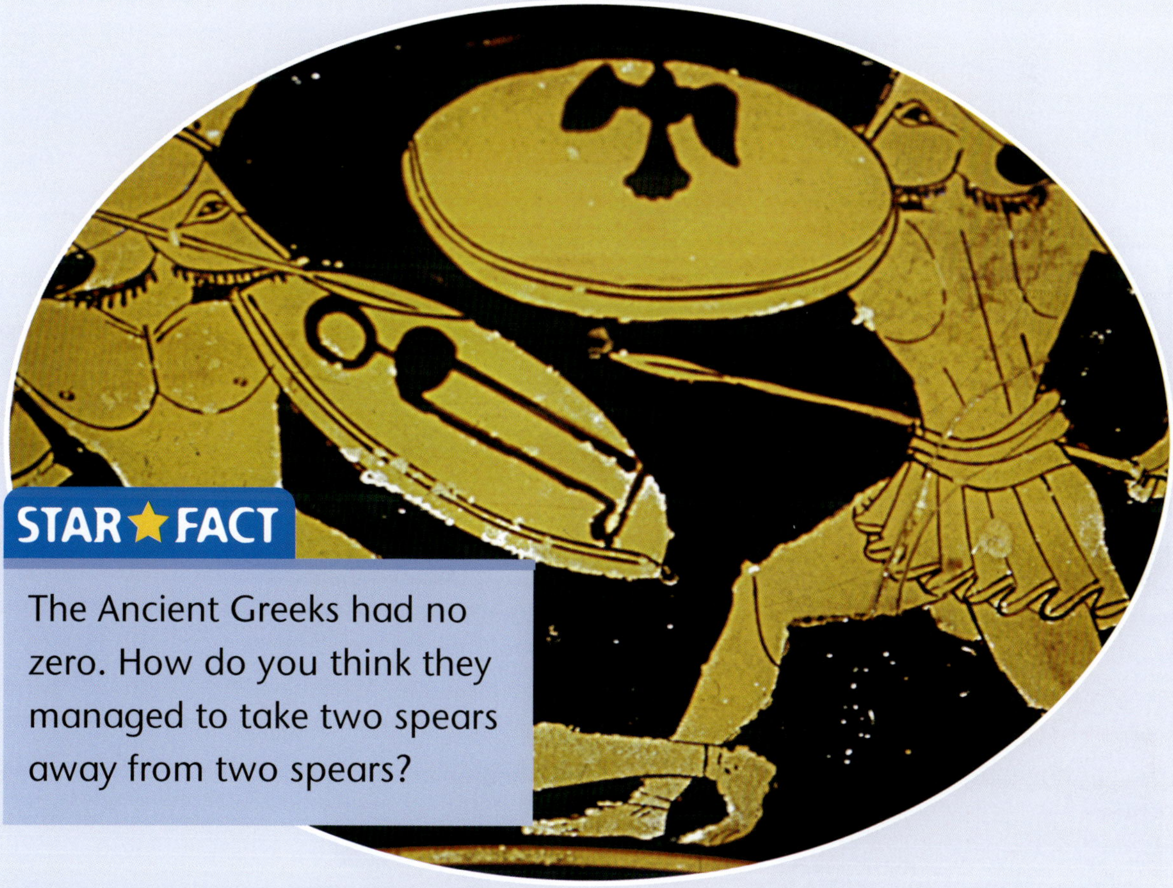

STAR ★ FACT

The Ancient Greeks had no zero. How do you think they managed to take two spears away from two spears?

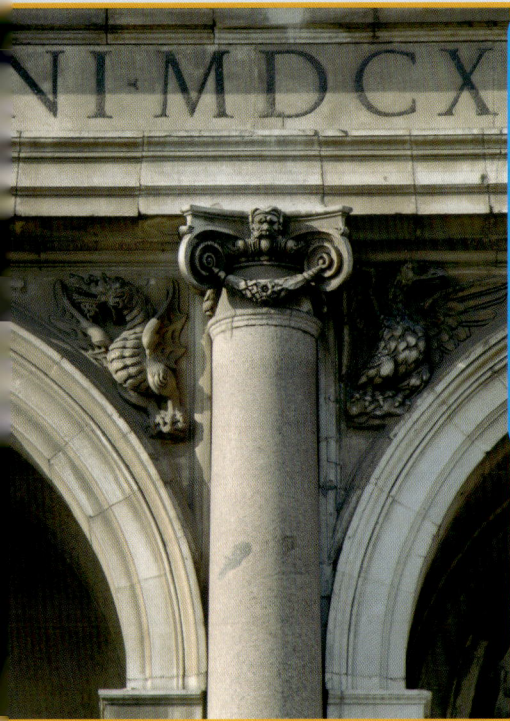

The Romans did not have many symbols for their numbers either. To write all the numbers up to 1000 they only had these symbols:

I = 1   V = 5   X = 10   L = 50
C = 100   D = 500   M = 1,000

If you put a lower number before a higher one, that means take away.
So IV = 5 − 1 = 4 and IL = 50 − 1 = 49
But if you put a lower number after a higher one, that means add.
So VI = 5 + 1 = 6 and LI = 50 + 1 = 51

What are these Roman numbers?
a DLV   **b** IC
What are these numbers in Roman numbers?
c 17   **d** 1,025

Answers below

a 555   **b** 99   **c** XVII   **d** MXXV
Answers

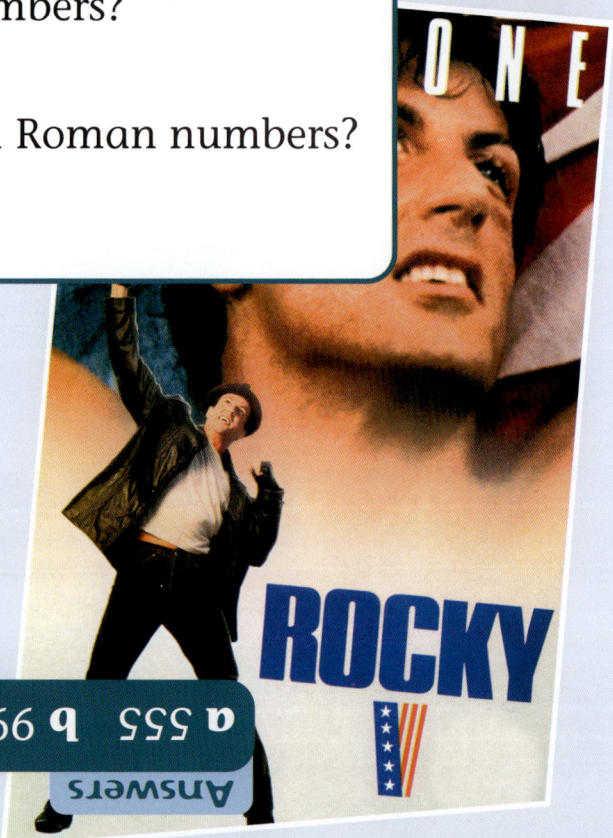

Where do you find Roman numbers today?

STAR ★ FACT

TV programmes often put the date they were made in Roman numerals at the end.

© BBCTV
MMII

When was this programme made?

Henry the 8th, or Henry VIII?

This stands for Elizabeth Regina (Queen) the Second.

Can you think of any other examples near where you live?

9

0	1	2	3	4	5	6	7	8	9
٠	١	٢	٣	٤	٥	٦	٧	٨	٩

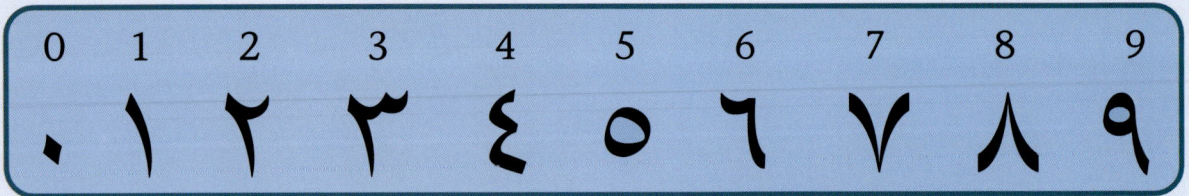

These Arabic numbers have been used for two thousand years.

STAR ★ FACT

Arabic is written from right to left, but numbers go from left to right.

41 = ٤١   What is the Arabic for 57 ?

Answer below

قطر
:١٧٥٨٤٠:

What is the number of this car? Look for the shapes of the numbers that you know.

Place value	Hundreds	Tens	Units
Arabic	٩	٢	٠
Our numbers	9	2	0

The numbers we use come from these Arabic numbers.

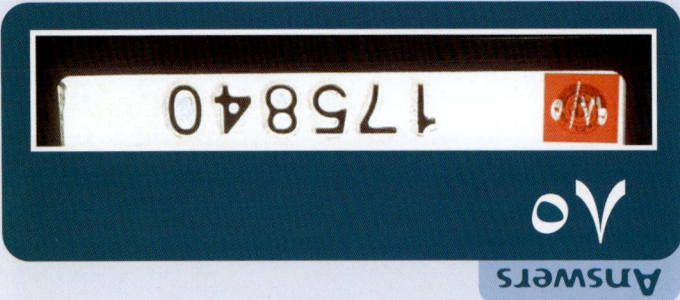

175840
٩٨/٩

٥٧
Answers

1	2	3	4	5	6	7	8	9
一	二	三	四	五	六	七	八	九

These are Chinese digits.

One	Two	Three	Four	Five	Six	Seven	Eight	Nine
壹	貳	叄	肆	伍	陸	柒	捌	玖

These are Chinese numbers.

拾	佰	仟	萬
10	100	1000	10,000

The Chinese also have special symbols for big numbers.

Can you see the numbers one, two and five on these notes?

What special symbol do we use when we want to say one thousand of something, e.g. 1,000 metres? 2,000 grammes?

Tally Ho!

Look back at how the Ancient Egyptians wrote numbers up to nine. We call these tally marks.

卌 = 5

To make it easier to add them up, you make tallies in lots of five.

Use tally marks when you are counting, keeping a score, or doing a questionnaire.

Try this questionnaire amongst your friends.

	Cartoon	Adventure	Spy	Animal
What kind of film do you like best?	卌 卌 |||	卌 |||	||	||||

You can then use these scores to make a bar chart.

Electronic numbers

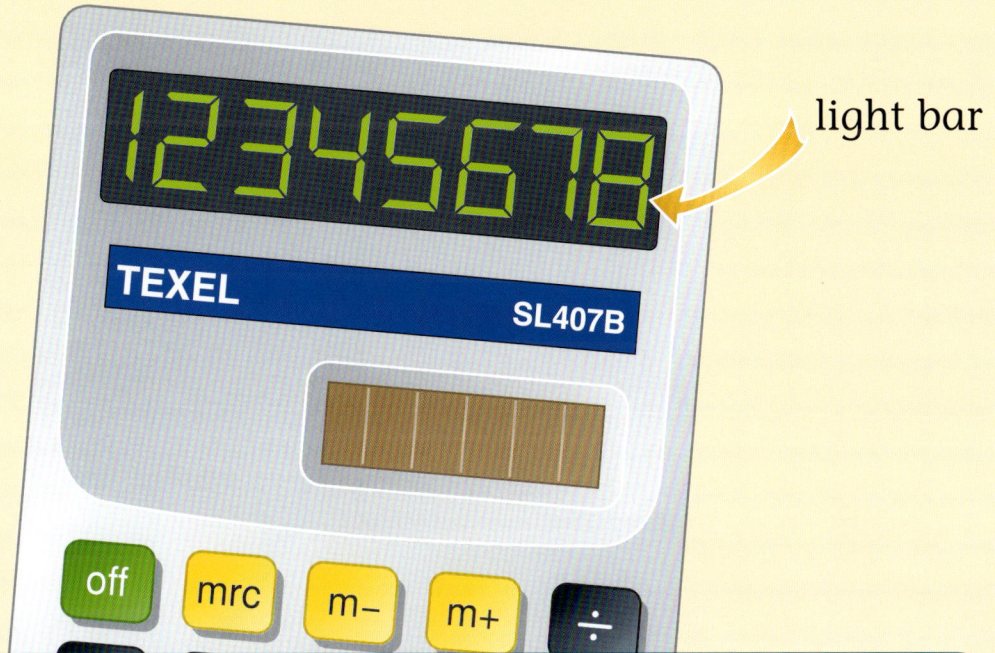

TEXEL

SL407B

off   mrc   m−   m+   ÷

Look at how numbers are made on a calculator.

There are seven light bars for each number.

Not all of them are used to make each number.

How many light bars are used to make these numbers?

a 0   **b** 888   **c** 102

d which three digit number uses the fewest light bars?

Answers below

Can you use a turtle or computer program like *logo* to make these calculator numbers?

Play Battleships

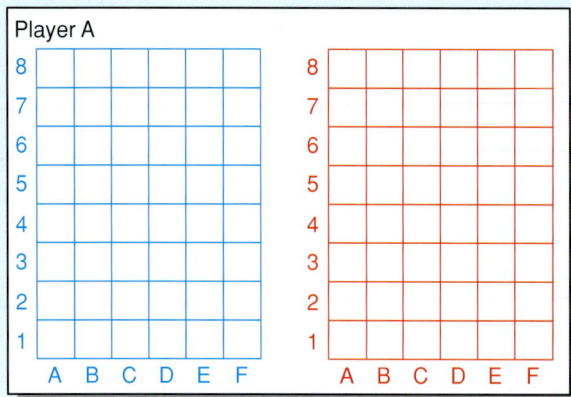

Player A

Player A

Player B

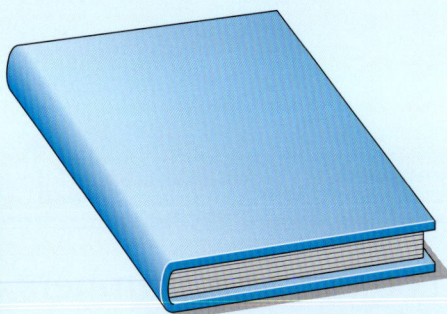

You will need

2 people

2 sheets of squared paper

pencils

2 books (to hide your paper)

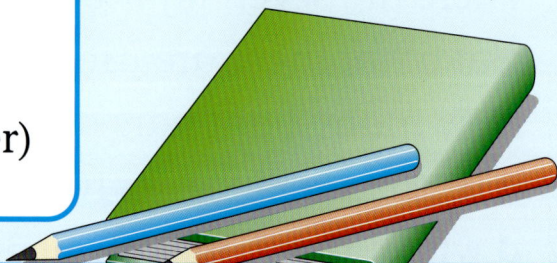

Before you start

- Draw a red and blue grid on each sheet.
- Draw each grid 6cm across and 8cm up.
- Label A– F across and 1 – 8 up, as shown on the picture.
- Hide your paper. On the red grid, draw one ship 3 squares long, two ships 2 squares long, and three ships 1 square long.

To play

Player A: Call out a grid reference (across then up), e.g. A1.

Player B: Check that reference on your red grid. If you have a ship, or part of a ship in that box say 'Hit!' if not, say 'Miss!'

Player A: Use the blue grid to find player B's ships. Mark the box you called on the blue grid with an × if it is a miss or a ✓ if it is a hit.

Player A: If it is a hit, take another turn.

Player B: If it is not a hit, you take a turn.

Player A

battleship
3 squares

destroyer
1 square

cruiser
2 squares

Keep swapping turns until one player has sunk all the other's ships.

No ship can be beside another. All the squares that a ship is on have to be hit before it is sunk.

15

Chess and mighty big numbers

There is a story that when an Indian mathematician invented chess, his king was so pleased that he offered to give the mathematician anything he asked for.

'Sire,' said the mathematician. 'Just give me some rice. Put one grain on the first square of my chessboard. Put two grains on the next square. Four grains on the next one, and keep on doubling the number of grains till you have covered all 64 squares.'

'Is that all?' cried the king.

BUT …

the king could not grant the wish. Why?

There are 64 squares on a chessboard.
1 + 1 = 2, 2 + 2 = 4, 4 + 4 = 8, 8 + 8 = 16 ...

Which square would be the first to have more than 1,000 grains on it? Use a calculator.

You would need to put 9,223,372,036,854,775,808 grains of rice on the last square.
The ruler would need to give the mathematician 18,446,744,073,709,551,615 grains of rice for the whole chessboard!

That number of grains of rice would fill a square 4 km cubed, or stretch to the nearest star, and back!

To infinity and beyond!

Digits have special values depending on their place in a number. You can write 123,456.789 using place value boxes, like this …

Hundred Thousands	Ten Thousands	Thousands	Hundreds	Tens	Units	Tenths	Hundredths	Thousandths
1	2	3	4	5	6 .	7	8	9

But did you know that the place values can stretch to infinity both ways? So the simple number ONE could be written like this …

OOOOOOOOOOOOOOOOOOOOOOOOOOOOOOOOOOOOOOOOO
OOOOOOOOOOOOOOOOOOOOOOOOOOOOOOOOOOOOOOOOO
OOOOOOOOOOOOOOOOOOOOOOOOOOOOOOOOOOOOOOOOO
OOOOOOOOOOOOOOOOOOOOOOOOOOOOOOOOOOOOOOOOO
OOOOOOOOOOOOOOOOOOO1 . OOOOOOOOOOOOOOOOO
OOOOOOOOOOOOOOOOOOOOOOOOOOOOOOOOOOOOOOOOO
OOOOOOOOOOOOOOOOOOOOOOOOOOOOOOOOOOOOOOOOO
OOOOOOOOOOOOOOOOOOOOOOOOOOOOOOOOOOOOOOOOO

Definition

Infinity: very great, something that goes on forever.

Imagine having to do that every time you have to write '1'.
(Don't do it! Your teacher will not be happy with us!)

$\frac{1}{3}$

One third seems like a simple number.

$\frac{1}{3}$

$\frac{1}{3}$

You can divide many things into three equal parts but some numbers are infinite – they just keep going. Try dividing one by three. You get …

0 . 33333333333333333333333333333333
33333333333333333333333333333333
33333333333333333333333333333333
33333333333333333333333333333333
33333333333333333333333333333333
33333333333333333333333333333333
33333333333333333333333333333

… and so to infinity.

Try doing it on your calculator.

Pick a number

Ask a friend to look at these grids. Ask them to pick a number, without telling you what it is. Ask them to tell you which grid, or grids, their number is in.

A

1	3	5	7	9
11	13	15	17	19
21	23	25	27	29
31	33	35	37	39
41	43	45	47	49

B

2	3	4	7	10
11	14	15	18	19
22	23	26	27	30
31	34	35	38	39
42	43	46	47	50

C

4	5	6	7	12
13	14	15	20	21
22	23	28	29	30
31	36	37	38	39
44	45	46	47	52

D

8	9	10	11	12
13	14	15	24	25
26	27	28	29	30
31	40	41	42	43
44	45	46	47	56

E

32	33	34	35	36
37	38	39	40	41
42	43	44	45	46
47	48	49	50	52
56				

F

16	17	18	19	20
21	22	23	24	25
26	27	28	29	30
31	48	49	50	52
56				

How to do the trick

To tell them what their number is add together all the numbers in the top left-hand corners of the grids your friend says their number is in.

So, for example if your friend chooses number 9 then they will point to these grids ...

A

1	3	5	7	9
11	13	15	17	19
21	23	25	27	29
31	33	35	37	39
41	43	45	47	49

D

8	9	10	11	12
13	14	15	24	25
26	27	28	29	30
31	40	41	42	43
44	45	46	47	56

Add together the first numbers in the grid and you get 1 + 8 = 9

Remember some numbers can be found in more than one grid

Map it

Numbers are very important on maps.

They can tell you:

- where you are.
- what road you're on.
- how high a mountain is. Brown numbers give the contour height.

Definition

Contour: A line on a map joining points that are the same height above sea level.

Look at the map of part of Scotland. The numbers in blue going along the map are Eastings. The numbers in blue going up the map are Northings.

A four-digit map reference for any square on a map gives a two-digit reference for the Eastings line to the *left* of the square and two-digit reference for the Northings line *below* the square. Square 38E 08N is pink on the map.

Look at this map.

1 Which water features can you find in square 40E 09N?

2 What is the number of the A road that goes through Fort Augustus?

3 How high (in metres) is Murligan Hill?

4 Can you give a four-digit map reference for Cherry Island?

STAR ★ FACT

Eastings go from East to West. They always start at a line that goes through the UK.

What else can numbers on a map tell you?

23

On the Equator

Map

S U D A N

Lokitaung•

E T H I O P I A

Lake Turkana

Chalbi Desert

Moyale•

S O M A L I A

Lodwar•

El Wak•

▲2293

•Marsabit

U G A N D A

Wajir•

Kerio

Ndoto Mountains

K E N Y A

▲2637

Lagh Bogal

▲3369
Maralal•

Ewsao Nyiro

Bungoma•

Nzoia

Equator

Kisumu•

Aberdare Range

▲5200
Mount Kenya

•Garissa

Nakuru•

•Embu

Kisii•

Tana

Narok•

Nairobi ■

Loita Hills

Magadi•

Athi

•Mutomo

Garsen•

Namanga•

Kibwezi•

Galana

Malinda•

T A N Z A N I A

Lake Victoria

INDIAN OCEAN

⊹
Mombasa

Key
- — International boundaries
- — Major roads
- — Railway
- ✈ Major airport
- ▲ Mountian peak (height in metres)
- ～ River
- 🌊 Lake

Land height (metres)
- above 5000
- 3000 – 5000
- 2000 – 3000
- 1000 – 2000
- 500 – 1000
- 300 – 500
- 200 – 300
- 100 – 200
- below 100

Sea depth (metres)
- 0 – 200
- 200 – 3000
- above – 3000

Scale
0   kilometres   500

Can you find the equator on the map?
Is the top of Mount Kenya north or south of the equator?
How high is Mount Kenya.

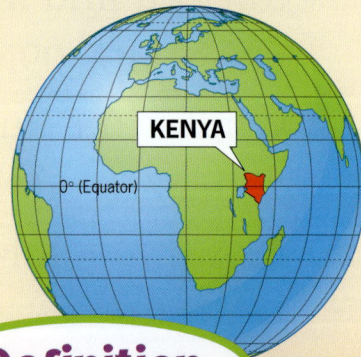

KENYA

0° (Equator)

Definition

Equator (say Ee-kway-ter): an imaginary line round the Earth at an equal distance from the North and South poles.